COPENHAGEN & DENMARK FOR TRAVELERS

-The total guide-

The comprehensive traveling guide for all your traveling needs.

© 2019 by **THE TOTAL TRAVEL GUIDE COMPANY**
© 2019 by **BRENDA PUBLISHING**

PUBLISHED BY

TABLE OF CONTENTS

WHY DO WE CLAIM OUR GUIDES ARE "TOTAL GUIDES"?

Why are they really comprehensive?

Because we do almost anything to make sure that all the main issues relevant to the conscious traveler are covered in our guides.

We hate the typical boring travel guides chocked up with standard information you can readily find on the Internet.

We travel, we research other guides, we talk to locals, we ask friends, we ask friends of friends,

we do whatever it takes to make sure that we have you covered. All the angles! This is how we get the best tips, the most valuable for every one of our travel destinations.

That is where we got the best tips, the most valuable ones about our travel destinations.

All our guides are reviewed and edited by a "local" writer to make sure that the guide is one of its kind, comprehensive, fun and interesting. We prefer not to add too many maps or photos since you can have all that on the internet. We prefer to focus the content on tips and unique data that makes worthwhile to buy our total guides.

We use different approaches for each city, as each destination is unique. You will be able to verify that our guides are not standardized. Each one is different because each place is different. And you will enjoy the difference,

Our production team is very proud of our guides. We hope you will enjoy the reading and take full advantage of your traveling.   !

INTRODUCTION

Copenhagen Mermaid Statue – Photo Source: pixabay.com

Copenhagen, the capital of Denmark, is a major point of attraction for tourists from all over the world. Approximately 8.7 million people come here each year, looking to discover the authentic Nordic culture and the Danish way of life. They are drawn to the beautiful, old buildings, the delicious food and the rich calendar of cultural events. Copenhagen is a city that is alive with passion, welcoming potential tourists with the slogan "Wonderful Copenhagen".

The majority of the tourists who come to Copenhagen also want to discover the other parts of Denmark. The whole country is beautiful to visit, with some of the most popular towns for visiting being Aalborg, Aarhus or Odense. Denmark is the country of fairytales, with Hans Christian Andersen making his influence felt event today. The Denmark Islands are especially wonderful to visit, with old monuments and castles enticing the travelers and increasing their thirst for adventure. As a tourist in Denmark, you always have something new to discover, whether it is related to culture, art or tradition. The Viking culture is also a powerful symbol of Denmark, whether it is reflected through the medieval festivals or the jewelry that reminds of times long gone.

The first chapter is dedicated to the reasons why you should visit Copenhagen and the rest of Denmark. As you will see for yourself, there are many great reasons that should bring you to this destination. You can then move on to the second chapter, in which I have provided local advice, gathered from my own experience living in Denmark. The third chapter contains information on how to travel to Copenhagen & Denmark on a budget; despite what everyone thinks, it is possible to come to this country and not spend a fortune during your trip. In the fourth chapter, I have included all the travel basics that you need to know, allowing you to organize your holiday to perfection.

In the fifth chapter, you will find information on the transportation system in Copenhagen and Denmark in general. From this chapter, you will understand that there are a lot of opportunities for transportation in this country. The sixth chapter is dedicated to the best hotels and restaurants that you can find here, while the next one contains valuable details on the cultural highlights. If you want to discover the best shopping opportunities of Copenhagen and Denmark, you will certainly read the eighth chapter. At the end of the book, you will find a short portrait of this amazing holiday destination. After reading this book, you would already have started to pack your bags for Copenhagen and Denmark!

WHY VISIT COPENHAGEN & DENMARK?

Copenhagen Water Canal – Photo Source: Pixabay.com

Copenhagen, the capital of Denmark, is a splendid choice for a holiday, surprising tourists with its rich culture, ancient heritage and cosmopolitan flair. If you have decided to visit Copenhagen and Denmark in general, you are in for a real treat. From the start, the Danish capital is going to enchant you with its amazing food, culture and hospitality. There are many reasons why you want to visit Copenhagen and some of them have been included in this chapter.

If you are into theme parks, one of the most important reasons why you should consider visiting Copenhagen is Tivoli (http://www.tivoli.dk; Vesterbrogade 3; +4533151001). This theme park is going to pleasantly surprise you with its 19th-century atmosphere but also with its modern rides and amazing restaurants. There are vintage Ferris wheels and colorful merry-go-rounds to be discovered, not to mention the beautiful Oriental Theatre, which dates from 1874. Here, you can see amazing ballet performances, listen to serenades and fall in love with the twinkling Chinese lanterns.

For those of you who love going to the beach, I can tell you that Copenhagen has one of the finest urban stretches of sand in the entire Europe. This is known as Amager Strandpark (http://www.amager-strandpark.dk; Amager Strandvej; +4533663319) and it is quite a popular choice among both tourists and local residents like myself. Many people use this location for bicycling or rollerblading but the majority comes for the sunbathing. However, I must warn you against swimming, as the water temperature is not as high as you might expect. You can satisfy your passion for swimming by choosing one of the outdoor swimming pools. One of the most recommended places for experiencing an authentic Scandinavian swim is Islands Brygge Havnebadet (http://teambade.kk.dk/indhold/havnebade-0; Islands Brygge 14; +4533663366).

In the past few years, Copenhagen has entered on the list of top European capitals that enjoy an excellent gastronomic reputation. The food served in Danish restaurants is amazing and you will certainly have the opportunity to discover that, during your stay in Copenhagen. Speaking about food, the Danish have a reputation for having some of most delicious pastry to be savored. However, if you find yourself in a bakery, avoid asking for a Danish - instead, order the wienerbrød and you will enjoy a traditional tasty treat. The best place to enjoy the wienerbrød is at La Glace (https://laglace.dk/en/), as this place has the same recipe since the 1870s. Together with a cup of coffee, it makes up for the perfect snack. You can also enjoy the delicious smørrebrød, which is actually sliced rye bread, topped with cold meat, smoked fish, cheese or even pate. For a lot of Danes, the smørrebrød is an excellent choice for lunch, as it will surely be for you.

Everywhere you go, you will see that the Danes are extremely friendly and welcoming. The Danish way of being is presented as "hygge", a word that does not have a correspondent in the English language but it stands for friendliness and coziness. This is also the way the Danes are coping with the short days during the cold season, meeting with their friends and enjoying long dinners, with home-cooked food and wine.

During your stay in Denmark, you have to use a bike, at least once. Copenhagen, as well as the other large towns of Denmark, is bike-friendly and you will see that the Danes take a lot of pride in their bikes. Many of them are adorned with unique details, representing in fact an extension of their personality.

Copenhagen has many times been compared to Venice, due to its numerous, beautiful canals. If you want to experience Copenhagen from a completely new perspective, you can take a canal tour. It is also recommended that you visit the canal quarter of Christianshavn, which is particularly beautiful. If you get lost, do not hesitate to ask for directions. You won't have any problems being understood, as more than 80% of the Danes are fluent in the English language.

For a completely different experience, you can visit Christiania (http://www.christiania.org/; Prinsessegade; +4532956507). Christiania is an alternative society, with its own rules, having been developed by a group of hippies in the 1970s.

The good news is that Denmark has events all year round, providing tourists who come here with a full calendar. Another advantage is that the country is small and compact, which makes it quite easy to travel from point to the other. Anywhere you will travel, you will discover people who are hospitable. In terms of leisure activities, there are plenty of great choices available. You can travel to Funen, the third largest island of Denmark, discovering its fairytale castles and walking on the streets where Hans Christian Andersen once lived. From there, you can go to Zealand and check out the beautiful historical sights, including the famous Kronborg Castle (http://www.kronborg.dk; Kronborg 2C, Helsingør; +4549213078). This castle is said to have inspired Shakespeare in writing Hamlet, so it is definitely worth a visit. If you have a passion for the Viking culture, you should check out the Viking sites that are located in Roskilde and Frederiksborg.

The beauty about Denmark is that you have the opportunity to discover cities that exude a small-town charm, no matter how big they are. Some of them will impress you with their natural setting, such as the beautiful Aarhus, which is nestled between fjords. Others, such as Odense, will make you feel like you have gone back in time.

In terms of culture, Denmark and Copenhagen have a lot of things to offer. There are world class museums that you visit, exhibits that are organized on a regular basis and music concerts all year long. Perhaps one of the most beautiful museums of Denmark is the underwater Maritime Museum (http://www.mfs.dk; Ny Kronborgvej 1, Helsingør; +4549210685). This has been named the European Museum of the Year 2015, so you may want to pay it a visit and see how beautiful it actually is.

Denmark, with its capital and the other beautiful areas, will seduce you, whether you will find yourself here for a brief visit or you will enjoy a longer stay. There are approximately 8700 km of beaches and holiday islands to discover, Viking camps and plenty of UNESCO World Heritage Sites to see. You can get active in one of the national parks of Denmark, enjoying activities such as cycling or discovering the most amazing diversity of watersports.

COPENHAGEN & DENMARK LOCAL TRAVEL ADVICE

If you have decided to travel to Copenhagen and Denmark in general, there are a few

Danish Bike – Photo Source: Pixabay.com

things that you should know first. Keep in mind that bicycles are often used as means of traveling and that you have to pay attention to cyclists, including when you are driving your car or walking the street. You should check your mirrors before turning right on a street, checking the bicycle lane out. Also, you should never walk on the bicycles lanes, as there are a lot of people who pedal at genuinely high speeds. Copenhagen has a free bike service that you can also use; you just have to deposit a small fee, which you will get when returning the bike.

Copenhagen has a lot of opportunities to offer in terms of transportation, including bio-fueled buses, smart cars and bicycles. The circulation in the Danish capital functions smoothly and there are no angry drivers to worry about. However, I must warn you about the fact that many of the streets in the city center have been pedestrianized, so you will not be able to use a car in that part of Copenhagen. For those of you who are coming here by car, as soon as you will enter the city, you will see that the sign says Greater Copenhagen. This is actually the modern capital, with all of its suburbs. But, if you want to visit traditional Copenhagen, you must go to the small waterway area that is found between Zealand and Amager. It is interesting to see how much the area of Greater Copenhagen has developed – for example, Frederiksberg is a town on its town but it is considered as being a part of this area.

In case you are wondering about the best time to visit, I recommend visiting Copenhagen and the rest of Denmark during the warm period, meaning from early May until late August. If you travel earlier in the spring, you might not enjoy the weather so much, while in autumn and winter, you might not feel so comfortable with the short days. The only exception is around the winter holidays, with the beautiful Christmas markets and the celebrations being perfect for a visit. The summer remains the ideal time to visit this amazing country, with many of the towns providing numerous opportunities for summer activities (you will especially enjoy the free swimming pools and the sandy beaches).

As it happens with anyone who travels for the first time to a new country, you might not feel so free to communicate with the locals. As a local myself, I must tell you that us, Danes, welcome tourists who come to visit our country. So, whether you find yourself in Copenhagen or in any other part of Denmark, do not hesitate to ask for directions. You will see that the locals are friendly and always happy to help tourists, speaking English quite well. If you are still having trouble finding certain tourist attractions, you can visit the official tourist agency, Wonderful Copenhagen, which is located near the main train station of Copenhagen. Here, you will discover an equally-friendly staff, speaking not only Danish and English, but many other languages as well. You can get a map of the town, ask for directions and even book your hotel using one of the PC terminals that are located there.

The good news is that the entrance to the most museums of Copenhagen and Denmark in general is free. However, you have to remember that all museums are closed one day per week, most commonly on Wednesdays. The majority of the museums provide information in English as well – nevertheless, if you want to be sure of this fact, you must check out their websites. Art enthusiasts should definitely consider paying a visit to the Danish National Gallery (http://www.smk.dk/; Sølvgade 48-50, Copenhagen; +4533748494). This is also free to visit, being closed each Monday of the week. Here, you have the opportunity to see some of the most beautiful works of renowned artists, such as Rembrandt, Picasso or Matisse.

If you want to see all of Copenhagen from above, you have to visit Rundetårn (http://www.rundetaarn.dk/; Købmagergade 52A, Copenhagen; +4533730373), an observation platform that can be reached by climbing the helical corridor of a tower that dates from the 17th Century. This is one of the oldest functioning observatories throughout Europe and you will certainly love the view.

In regard to the Internet access, you should know that public libraries provide such services. However, the free Internet access is limited to one hour and one has to sign up for it in advance. You can also use the Internet at one of the cheap Internet cafes that are found near the central station of Copenhagen or connect to the Wi-Fi hotspots that are located throughout the town (and in other Danish towns as well). On the S-train, the Wi-Fi connection is free, so this can be quite a useful information to known when traveling.

It would be a lie to say that Copenhagen and Denmark in general are not expensive as travel destinations. If you are planning on visiting this part of Europe at the peak season, you will need to up your budget. This is why I recommend coming here off-season, avoiding the crowded summer. However, as you will see in the following chapter, it is possible to come here when you are on a tight budget as well. I will teach you everything there is to know about traveling to Copenhagen and Denmark on a budget, so no worries about that.

If you are planning on visiting the Faroe Islands as well, you need to be careful during the whaling season (between June and September), as there are some security concerns related to the protesters who come here.

The Danes are not only friendly but they are also very polite, taking pride in the respect that they offer to one another. For example, if you are standing in line, make sure that you do not skip in front of another person. This is considered extremely rude and you will certainly do not want to create the wrong impression about yourself. Also, if you want to get more acquainted with locals such as myself, you can use the Meet the Danes Service (http://www.meetthedanes.dk/). This is actually a service that arranges for home dinners, allowing you to come in contact with a Danish family.

COPENHAGEN AND DENMARK ON A BUDGET

Copenhagen Rooftop - Photo Source: pixabay.com

Even though both Copenhagen and Denmark have a reputation for being expensive, this is not necessarily true. Yes, the sales tax in Denmark is impressive – 25%. Yes, there are plenty of shops, hotels and restaurants that seem to have been made for kings. But, with the right moves, you can enjoy Copenhagen and the best of Denmark on a budget. Let's see how you can actually do that.

First of all, you need to visit the website of the Danish Rail System – http://www.dsb.dk/ - and discover the orange tickets. These are tickets that you can actually print and use them for train transportation. The advantage? These are really cheap, approximately 1/3 from what the regular tickets cost. Speaking about the train and bus transportation, you should know that you can also benefit from discounted rides (up to 50%), by booking your tickets with at least one month in advance. Apart from that, you can travel around Copenhagen or other towns of Denmark, taking advantage of the free bike service (make sure that you do not forget about the 20 kroner as deposit).

In regard to the food, it is recommended that you cook your own food and purchase groceries from the supermarket. Eating out isn't cheap, especially when it comes to dinner and particularly in Copenhagen. If you do insist to eat out, do it at lunch, where there are many specials and buffet deals that you can take advantage of.

There is always the possibility of enjoy the street food – in Copenhagen, as well as in other towns of Denmark, there are varied choices that can be savored, while saving money. You can enjoy American-style hot dogs, sausages of all kinds, traditional sandwiches, kebabs and pizza at genuinely discounted prices. Money can be saved as well by drinking tap water, instead of buying the expensive bottled kind. Keep in mind that Denmark has some of the cleanest waters in the world, so it is 100% safe to drink tap water.

When it comes to accommodation, you will find Copenhagen and the rest of Danish towns to offer different opportunities, suitable to all budgets. If you are looking for cheap or even free accommodation, you could always try out couchsurfing (http://www.couchsurfing.com/). The one thing that you have to keep in mind is that the request has to be sent far in advance. Other cheap accommodation opportunities include hostels (commonly known as Danhostels here), renting a caravan or a summerhouse (especially during the off season) and pitching your tent at the forest or at the beach. There is one more opportunity that you should be aware of – by visiting http://www.airbnb.com, you can find people who are willing to rent their homes to potential tourists at affordable rates.

For the time spent in the Danish capital, you can also consider purchasing the Copenhagen Card. This is similar to the tourist cards that are available in other European cities, providing free admission to no less than 74 museums and attractions. Apart from that, for the duration of the card, you can benefit from free public transportation (metro, train and bus). The tourist card offers discounts for different restaurants, car rental services and other sights. Both adults (16+) and kids (10-15) can benefit from the Copenhagen Card; also, if you have children under ten, you can take them on your card (benefitting from free entry as well).

The price of the Copenhagen Card varies according to its duration: 24 hours – 359 DKK (adults) and 189 DKK (kids); 48 hours – 499 DKK (A) and 249 DKK (K); 72 hours – 589 DKK (A) and 299 DKK (K); 120 hours – 799 DKK (A) and 399 DKK (K). Among the attractions that you are granted free admission to, there are: Tivoli Amusement Park (http://www.tivoli.dk/; Vesterbrogade 3; +4533151001), Canal Tours (http://www.stromma.dk; Nyhavn 3; +4532963000), Rundetårn (http://www.rundetaarn.dk; Købmagergade 52A; +4533730373), Copenhagen Zoo (http://www.zoo.dk/; Roskildevej 32; +4572200200), Kronborg Slot (http://www.kronborg.dk; Krongborg 2C; +4549213078), Det Nationalhistoriske Museum (http://www.dnm.dk/; Frederiksborg Slot; +4548260439) and Experimentarium City (http://www.experimentarium.dk; Trangravsvej 10-12; +4539273333).

Interestingly enough, you can purchase the tourist card before your actual travel, receiving them by mail or as a voucher by email. If you want, you can order the tourist cards from home and pick them up, either at the 3rd terminal of the

COPENHAGEN & DENMARK FOR TRAVELERS

Copenhagen airport or at the Copenhagen Tourist Agency. The card becomes valid from the first time you show it in a museum or in a bus (or other means of transportation). You can visit each attraction once in 24 hours – if you have chosen a card that has a longer validity, the number of allowed visits per attraction can extend to three (72 hours card) or to five (120 hours card). Keep in mind that these tourist cards are also sold at hotels.

There are many free events that you can attend during your stay in Copenhagen and Denmark. Among the most popular, there are: Aalborg Carnival (http://www.aalborgkarneval.dk/), Aarhus University Beer Relay (http://www.visitaarhus.com/ln-int/central-jutland/events-students) and Gay Pride Parade (http://www.copenhagenpride.dk/). Apart from the events, there are numerous free attractions to check out, not only in Copenhagen but also in other parts of Denmark as well. You can visit the famous white cliffs of Mø, climb the enormous migrating dune of Råbjerg Mile and check out the fossil records of Stevns Klint. If you have a passion for the Viking culture, you can go to Trelleborg and check out the Museum of the Viking Age (http://natmus.dk/museerne/trelleborg), which is part of the National Museum of Denmark.

A part of the Viking culture can also be discovered by visiting the rune stones at Jelling (this was the first UNESCO World Heritage Site of Denmark). From there, you can go to Rubjerg Knude Fyr and see the famous lighthouse that is slowly swallowed by the sand dunes. Bookworms will certainly take delight in visiting Assistens Churchyard (http://assistens.dk/), the place where the famous Hans Christian Andersen and Søren Kierkegaard are resting.

If you are looking to re-connect with nature, you can benefit from a free holiday on an ecological farm. By visiting http://www.wwoof.dk, you can be part of the program that is known as Willing Workers on Organic Farms. Basically, you are offered free boarding and food in exchange for the farm work. In Denmark, you can also pitch your tent at one of the free camping sites. Online, on the website of the Danish Nature Agency (http://eng.naturstyrelsen.dk/), you download a map with all the camping sites of Denmark, including the wild ones (marked with green).

COPENHAGEN AND DENMARK TRAVEL BASICS

Sunset in Denmark - Photo Source: pixabay.com

As a tourist traveling to Denmark, you should know that this country is relatively safe. However, during the peak season, you will need to protect yourself against pickpockets, especially in areas where there are a lot of tourists. Whenever you find yourself in a crowded area, make sure that you do not flash any expensive equipment around and that you keep your personal belongings secure (including your ID or passport and money). Late at night, you might want to avoid the areas of Christiania and Nørrebro, as the locals living there can get quite violent, especially when confronting with the authorities.

In regard to driving a car between the different towns of Denmark, you should know that the road conditions are excellent. When driving, you must keep your lights on and always wear the seatbelt. In Copenhagen and other big towns of Denmark, you have to pay increased attention to cyclists, especially when changing lanes or turning at the corner of the street.

If you are coming from countries outside Europe, you require a visa in order to enter Denmark. The visa is not required for those who come from countries that are members of the European Union. In case you are planning for a longer stay in Denmark or Copenhagen, you will need to acquire a resident permit. Also, keep in mind that Greelannd and the Faroes are not in the European Union. When it comes to health issues, you can purchase travel insurance (covering medical needs as well) or get the free European Health Insurance Card (covers medical emergencies, valid in Greeland and Faroes as well).

You can arrive in Copenhagen by plane, landing at the Kastrup Airport. At this airport, you will see flights from international carriers but also low-cost flights. The train from Kastrup International Airport to the Central Station of Copenhagen takes approximately 12 minutes. You can also consider the Sturup Airport – this is located in Malmø (Sweden) but it is only half an hour from Copenhagen. Denmark can also be reached by train – the railway system is extremely well developed, allowing you to travel between Copenhagen and the rest of the country. Ferry transportation is also possible, allowing you to travel to Sweden and Norway.

Even though Denmark is a member of the European Union, its currency is the Danish Krone. However, many restaurants and hotels accept other currencies as well, such as the Swedish Kronor and Euro. You can go to the bank or to an exchange office to change money – in the past few years, the exchange offices have become widespread and they offer decent rates. You have to pay attention to the commission – if they require such a thing, it is usually written in a small print and you need to check it out. Avoid the area of Strøget in Copenhagen, as the rates are usually low and the commission high. Using the exchange machines is not recommended, as the associated fees can be quite high.

In Copenhagen and Denmark in general, the major credit cards are accepted. However, you have to be careful, as there are a lot of supermarkets and small shops that accept only Danish credit cards (these are known as Dankort). You can use your international credit card at one of those ATMs and obtain the cash you need.

As it was already mentioned, the Danes speak English fluently but it might not hurt to learn a few useful Danish phrases, such as: "Velkommen" (welcome), "Hej" (Hello), "God morgen" (Good Morning), "God nat" (Good night), "Hej Hej" (Goodbye).

The time zone is Denmark is GMT+1. If you are coming from countries that have a different time zone, you might experience jet lag and need a few days to accommodate. Also, you might require a specific adaptor plug for the electrical appliances. There are no special health risks or vaccination requirements for Denmark; however, during the summer season, you might want to protect yourself against the ticks, especially if you will travel in areas where there is a lot of vegetation. You will also need to purchase the travel insurance, making sure that you are covered for health problems as well. It is for the best that you choose a policy that covers different areas, including the one that offers protection in case of theft (this is especially valid for those who are traveling with expensive camera equipment).

These is some basic information that can help you plan your trip to Copenhagen and Denmark. Read the chapter with increased attention and make sure that you organize your to-do list, based on the information provided.

TRANSPORTATION IN COPENHAGEN AND DENMARK

The public transportation in Copenhagen is defined by reliability, punctuality and

Bike Parking in Copenhagen - Photo Source: pixabay.com

coverage, taking you everywhere you want to go in the town. The good news is that, like in other European capitals, you can use the same ticket for different methods of transportation, including the train, metro, bus and even waterbus. The metro is especially useful, as it allows you the opportunity to travel directly from the airport to the center of Copenhagen.

The bus transportation service is quite well-developed, being used by both tourists and locals like myself. First, you have the A-buses, which cover the transportation in the center of Copenhagen. These are available at every 3-7 minutes during the busiest times of the day (morning and afternoon); after the rush hour has passed,

25

they run every 10 minutes. The A-buses are available at all hours of the day or night, so you don't have to worry about not finding transportation late at light.

The S-buses run every 5-10 minutes when there is the highest demand and, outside rush hour, every 20 minutes. Even though these buses are only available between 6 am and 10 pm, they are preferred by some people, due to the fact that they are faster than the A-buses (fewer stops). During the night, meaning between 1 and 5 am, you can always rely on the night buses (these are generally known as the N-buses). As for the bus stops, these are easily to recognize, due to the grey color with which they are marked.

The metro service is also available day and night, no matter the day of the week. During the busiest times of the day, the trains run at every 2-4 minutes; after the rush hour has passed, the trains run every 3-6 minutes (this time frame is also valid for the weekends). On Friday and Saturday night, after 1 am, the trains run every 7-15 minutes. Also, on the weekdays, the trains run every 20 minutes, after the midnight has passed. It should also be noted that the scheduled maintenance that takes place each and every night can delay your journey. This maintenance of the rails commonly takes place between 1-1.25 am and 4.15-4.45 am.

The S-train runs every day, between 5 am and 00.30 am. The S-train has several lines, including: line F (every 4-5 minutes), line A, B, C and E (every 10 minutes) and line H, Bx (every 20 minutes). You should keep in mind that, on Friday and Saturday, between 1-5 am, the trains run once per hour. However, during these hours, you also have available the line F, running every half hour.

No matter the type of public transportation you decide to use in Copenhagen, it is for the best that you buy the ticket before boarding the train, metro or bus. The tickets can be bought at automated machines that are found in the main stations, at kiosks that sell varied products and also at the DSB Ticket Office (you can find one at the airport or in the central station). You can also buy a ticket from the driver but you will require exact change for that. Keep in mind that traveling without a valid ticket will get you a fine of 750 DKK.

For the rest of Denmark, the transport infrastructure is just as well developed and tourists have plenty of opportunities for getting around. The methods of transportation include the plane, train, bus and personal car, with Denmark having an impressive 2600 km of railway and over 70000 km of road (out of which 1100 km are actually the motorway). Cycling is also a common method of transportation; it is estimated that there are over 4 million bikes throughout Denmark and over 10000 km of cycle routes to be covered. Many cities provide locals and tourists with the opportunity of using bikes for free (as you have seen above, all you need is a small fee to be used as deposit).

The bus service is a great idea if you want to reach the more remote parts of Denmark. Other from that, the long distance buses can be used in order to travel from Copenhagen to other Danish cities, such as Odense, Aarhus and Aalborg. When it comes to air traveling, you should know that Denmark has no less than 23 airports, out of which 5 are international. The two main airports of Denmark are Copenhagen and Billund. Daily flights leave Copenhagen and reach the main cities of Denmark. For example, SAS has direct flights to the cities of Aarhus, Aalborg and Billund, while Norwegian has flights to Aalborg, Billund and Karup.

The islands of Denmark are either connected to the main continent through bridges or they can be reached with the help of the ferry. One of the most renowned bridges is the one between Sealand and Funen, with a length of 17 km. The ferry remains a perfectly good transportation alternative for all those who want to reach Sealand, Funen or Jutland.

In regard to the train travel, you should know that the Danish rail operator DSB has numerous routes available all over Denmark and even in the southern part of Sweden. The journey with the train is pleasant and it allows you to discover the beautiful nature of Denmark. From Copenhagen to Aarhus, the journey takes three hours, to Aalborg four hours and to Odense only half an hour. On the website of DSB – http://www.dsb.dk/ - you can find all the information you need on train routes, schedules and even book your train tickets. The website has an English version and a very useful tutorial on how to use the booking system.

There are also special passes that you can use in order to benefit from discounted travels, such as the Eurail Denmark Pass (recommended for non-European travelers) and the InterRail Denmark Pass (indicated for European citizens). Online, at http://www.rejseplanen.dk/, you can plan your entire journey in Denmark, combining different methods of transportation.

BEST HOTELS AND RESTAURANTS

Interior Hall, Denmark Hotel - Photo Source: pixabay.com

When it comes to hotels, Copenhagen and Denmark have some pretty interesting to present to its visitors. There are lovely choices to be discovered, with prices suitable to all budgets. Let's check out where you should stay in Copenhagen and also in the rest of Denmark.

These are the best hotels of the Danish capital:

1. 71 Nyhavn Hotel

- Cozy and compact

- The hotel is located in a converted spice warehouse
- Located near the Nyhavn canal
- Special rates on the weekend
- Splendid view over the port
- Both standard rooms and duplex suites available
- Address: Nyhavn 71
- Tel.: +4533436200
- Website: http://www.71nyhavnhotel.dk/

2. Avenue

- Located on the beautiful Åboulevard avenue
- Elegant rooms
- Oasis of relaxation, starting with the fashionable lounge
- Standard rooms and suites available
- Family rooms with four beds
- Breakfast included in the room rate
- Address: Åboulevard 29, Frederiksberg
- Tel.: +4535373111
- Website: http://www.avenuehotel.dk/

3. Copenhagen Island Hotel

- Close to the Central Station of Copenhagen
- Located on a man-made island
- Minimalist Scandinavian style decoration
- Generous number of rooms (suites also available)
- Splendid views of the harbor
- Address: Kalvebod Brygge 53
- Tel.: +4533389600

- Website: http://www.copenhagenisland.dk/

4. Ibsens Hotel

- Budget-friendly hotel
- Located in a bohemian neighborhood (between the lakes and Nørrebro Station)
- The rooms are decorated in the modern Danish style
- Best choice – corner suites
- Discounted day passes for the spa located next to the hotel
- Electric cars and bikes available for hire
- Excellent breakfast buffet (included in the room rate) and free Wi-Fi
- Address: Vendersgade 23
- Tel.: +4533131913
- Website: http://www.arthurhotels.dk/ibsens-hotel/

5. Nimb

- Beautiful, small hotel
- Impeccably furnished rooms (13 available)
- Each room has a fireplace and a splendid view (over the Tivoli Gardens)
- Elegant cocktail lounge
- Wine cellar
- Close to the central station
- Address: Bernstorffsgade 5
- Tel.: +4588700000
- Website: http://www.nimb.dk/

These are the best hotels in Denmark:

1. Hotel Legoland

- Appeals to both grown-ups and children
- 223 rooms available

- Standard and family rooms
- Recommended choice – themed rooms (knight, princess, pirate and kingdom)
- The parking, buffet breakfast and park admission included in the room rates
- Address: Aastvej 10, 7190, Billund
- Tel.: +4579511350
- Website: http://www.legoland.dk/

2. Hotel Royal

- Luxury hotel
- Located in an elegant building (dating from 1838)
- Also has a casino, nightclub and garden restaurant
- Impressive interior decorations (all rooms with antique furniture)
- The dishes are prepared in the restaurant only from local, fresh produce
- Located at a close distance from Skolebakken Train Station and Aarhus Harbor
- Address: Store Torv 4, 8000 Aarhus
- Tel.: +4586120011
- Website: http://www.hotelroyal.dk/

3. Stammershalle Badehotel

- Located on the shore of Bornholm Island
- Charming hotel
- Splendid views over the Baltic Sea and Christiansø Island
- The gourmet restaurant has dishes prepared from local produce
- Free access to sauna and swimming pool
- Access to tennis court
- Bicycle rental
- Free private parking
- Address: Søndre Strandvej 128, 3760 Gudhjem
- Tel.: +4556484210

- Website: http://www.stammershalle-badehotel.dk/

4. Hotel Ærø

- Located at a close distance from the ferry docks
- The rooms are light and airy, being decorated in a modern fashion
- British-colonial style
- Pay extra for a room with a harbor view
- Free private parking for all guests
- Address: Vestergrade 38, 5970 Ærøskøbing
- Tel.: +4562521003
- Website: http://www.aeroehus.dk/

5. Hotel Randers

- One of the oldest hotels in Denmark
- Rich décor, each room is individualized
- Best choice – antique room
- Complimentary breakfast
- Free Wi-Fi connection
- Address: Torvegade 11, 8900 Randers
- Tel.: +4586423422
- Website: http://www.hotel-randers.dk/.

As for the restaurants, Denmark, together with its fine capital, has some of the best choices for eating out. Both local and international cuisine is served in elegant restaurants, guaranteeing an unforgettable dining experience. Let's check out the best restaurants of Copenhagen and Denmark.

These are the best restaurants of Copenhagen:

1. Restaurant Cofoco

COPENHAGEN & DENMARK FOR TRAVELERS

- Menu option – three to five courses (fixed price)
- Wide range of cuisine choices (French, Italian, South American and Nordic)
- Excellent wine menu
- Recommended to book the table in advance
- Affordable eating options
- Address: Abel Cathrines Gade 7
- Tel.: +4533136060
- Website: http://www.cofoco.dk/

2. Neighbourhood

- Best place to taste organic gourmet pizza
- Modern interpretation of the classic Italian pizza
- Interesting toppings – fresh salads, pickled veggies, fresh herbs, roasted sea food or meat
- Cocktails made from organic fine spirits
- Address: Istedgrade 27
- Tel.: +4532122212
- Website: http://www.neighbourhood.dk/

3. Restaurant Kjøbenhavn

- Located in the heart of Copenhagen
- Relaxing and welcoming atmosphere
- Danish quality food
- Renovated in 2015 (Copenhagen art by Paul Fischer on the walls)
- Three menus – 3, 5 and 7 servings (name of the menus – Bycyklen, Strøget and Kanalrundfarten)
- Address: Dronningens, Tværgade 10
- Tel.: +4522446666

- Website: http://kjobenhavn.dk/

4. La Galette

- French restaurant, located in the city center
- Charming atmosphere
- Recommended choice – pancakes with a wide range of fillings (salmon, spinach, cheese, goat cheese, ratatouille, ham)
- Dessert pancakes available as well (filled with chocolate, flamed calvados, candy apples or chestnut crème)
- Address: Larsbjørnsstræde 9
- Tel.: +4533323790
- Website: http://www.lagallette.dk/

5. Marv & Ben

- Located on Snaregade, the beautiful medieval street of Copenhagen
- Innovative regional cooking
- Best place to taste haute cuisine
- The menus change according to the season
- The dishes are prepared from local, fresh produce
- Address: Snaregade 4
- Tel.: +4533910191
- Website: http://www.cargocollective.com/marvogben/RESTAURANTEN.

These are the best restaurants in the rest of Denmark:

1. Kähler Villa Dining

- Perfect choice for dinner
- Excellent selection of aperitifs, appetizers and snacks

- Three course dinner, with unlimited wine and coffee
- Best gourmet restaurant in Aarhus
- Open view to the kitchen
- Unique Nordic culinary experience
- Mandatory advanced booking
- Address: Grenåvej 127, Risskov, Aarhus
- Tel.: +4586177088
- Website: http://www.villadining.dk/

2. Duus Vinkælder

- Perfect place to enjoy a traditional Danish meal
- Excellent wine selection
- Restaurant set in a beautiful cellar, with vaulted ceilings
- The building dates from 1624
- The servings are quite generous
- Traditional lunch and dinner buffet also available
- Address: Østerågade 9, Aalborg
- Tel.: +4598125056
- Website: http://www.duusvinkælder.dk/

3. Under Lindetræet

- Located right next to H.C. Andersen House
- The restaurant is set in an old building, beautifully preserved
- Gourmet restaurant
- National and international dishes available
- Address: Ramsherred 2, 5000 Odense
- Tel.: +4566129286
- Website: http://www.underlindetraet.dk/

4. Sushi Taro

- Amazing sushi restaurant
- Recommended choice – chef family menu
- Located in a beautiful building
- Tasty food at a great price
- Booking ahead is recommended on the weekends
- Address: Stengade 4B, 3000 Helsingør
- Tel.: +4549211200
- Website: http://www.sushitaro.dk/

5. Restaurant Gammelhavn

- Beautiful view over the harbor
- Friendly staff and relaxed atmosphere
- Recommended choice – season or sampler menu
- Affordable prices
- Address: Britanniavej 3, 6700 Esbjerg
- Tel.: +4576119000
- Website: http://www.gammelhavn.dk/.

TOP CULTURAL HIGHLIGHTS

Denmark Medieval Festival - Photo Source: pixabay.com

The cultural calendar of Copenhagen is filled to the maximum, with a wide range of events being organized each and every year. If you are planning on visiting Copenhagen in the near future, you should know that summer is one of the busiest times of the year, with plenty of events to attend.

The Copenhagen Fashion Festival (http://www.copenhagenfashionfestival.com/) is a must for anyone who is a fashion enthusiast. Organized twice a year – one week in February and one in August – this festival transforms Copenhagen into the Mecca of fashion. There are varied fashion events that you can attend, including trendy exhibitions, street parties and mini concerts. You can take part in different competitions, check out trend shows and enjoy the shopping events offering amazing discounts to an incredible variety of clothing items.

If music is more your thing, perhaps you might be interested in the Copenhagen Jazz Festival (http://www.jazz.dk/). This is considered one of the biggest jazz events in all of Europe, with over 250000 people attending each year. Organized in the summer, it transforms Copenhagen into a city of music, with jazz being heard on the streets and in the main squares of the city. You can listen to renowned artists performing in jazz clubs or in concert halls, taking part in what is also one of the oldest festivals in the city. This year's festival marks the 37th edition, so it should be quite interesting.

Speaking about music, there are two other events that you might be interested in, taking place in Copenhagen as well. The first is represented by the Copenhagen Opera Festival (http://www.copenhagenoperafestival.com/). This is not the ordinary opera festival that you might have seen or attended in other cities of Europe, as the opera performances are taken out of the traditional theatre. Instead, you have the opportunity to listen to some amazing artists, performing on the streets, underground and even on the waterways.

The second musical event is the Copenhagen Summer Festival (http://www.copenhagensummerfestival.dk/). Organized between the 27th of July and the 7th of August, it gives one the change to listen to classical chamber concerts. These take place in the Charlottenborg mansion, located in the center of Copenhagen and more specifically in Kongens Nytorv. The building itself is a delight to see, being built in the Dutch Baroque style. The interesting thing about this festival is that you get to listen to young musical talents performing in combination with established musicians.

For those of you have a passion for cooking and food in general, one of the most interesting events is Copenhagen Cooking (http://www.copenhagencooking.dk/). This is indeed one of the biggest cooking festivals that is organized in the northern part of Europe, paying a homage to the amazing culture of food. The festival lasts for approximately ten days in August, providing you with the opportunity to taste some pretty amazing dishes belonging to the Nordic cuisine.

And if you really want to be part of a colorful and festive event, you have to check out the Copenhagen Pride (http://www.copenhagenpride.dk/). Organized in August as well, it brings the LGBT community in the center of attention. Apart from the political message, this is also a time of celebration and all the events that are organized during this period are free to attend. If you want to show your support for the LGBT community, there are special bracelets that you can purchase and wear on your hand. During the Copenhagen Pride Week, the City Hall Square transforms into the Pride Square, being the focal point for this event. There are a lot of parties organized, not to mention music concerts and films.

As you have seen for yourself, Copenhagen has many events that you can attend, especially in the summer. However, you must be aware that the calendar of events is just as rich in the rest of Denmark. So, if you are planning on touring the country, there are many nice events to check out. Let's see the most important ones.

Culture and music come together at the Roskilde Festival (http://www.roskilde-festival.dk/), making this festival one of the largest events of its kind organized in the northern part of Europe. Over 80000 people attend the festival each year, being drawn not only to the music but also to the idea of camping on the site. For us, Danes, this festival represents a rite of passage. For tourists, the party atmosphere is fascinating. The tickets for the Roskilde Festival can be purchased online at http://www.billetnet.dk, providing you with access at both the festival site and camping area. Also, you should keep in mind that this festival is organized by an non-profit organization, all proceeds from the event going to charity.

The NorthSide Music Festival (http://www.northside.dk/) is an interesting event to check out, taking place each June in the town of Aarhus. By going to this music festival, you have the opportunity to see the live performance of both national and international artists. This is often presented as an innovative festival, due to the fact that its main focus is on the sustainability issues. It should be noted that the festival takes place in the center of Aarhus, as there is no camping site available. However, there are plenty of nice hotels in the town, providing comfortable accommodation.

Aarhus is often the scene of cultural events, with the Aarhus Festival (http://www.aarhusfestuge.dk/) being one of the most popular, among tourists and local residents like myself. This is one of the largest events that takes place in Scandinavia and each year it has a different theme, providing one with the change to see the performances of both international and national artists. The theme for 2015 is light – for this reason, you will see an amazing display of lighting, including with giant white rabbits that are illuminated from the inside.

The SPOT Festival (http://www.spotfestival.dk/) takes place in Aarhus as well, representing in fact a promotion platform for both Danish and Nordic music. The festival is organized with the purpose of supporting new bands or artists but you will also be able to see established artists performing. Interestingly enough, the festival provides participants with the opportunity to watch different movies, in which music is the main theme.

If you are a fan of Hans Christian Andersen, you must attend the festival dedicated to the famous writer, which is organized annually in Odense. The Hans Christian Andersen Festival (http://www.hcafestivals.com/) includes no less than 270 events, out of which 250 are free to attend. It represents the perfect place to re-discover the world of fairytales as an adult and a great joy for children. During a single weeks, in all the major squares of Odense, there are cabaret events and concerts, transforming the town in a place of imagination and adventure. Surely, the parade is the highlight of the event, with children having the opportunity to see their favorite characters coming to life.

Odense is also home to a unique event, meaning the Odense Flower Festival (http://www.blomsterfestival/dk). Organized between 13th and 16th of August, it represents the perfect choice for those who are passionate about the world of flowers. In 2015, the flower festival is dedicated to Carl Nielsen, one of the greatest music composers of Denmark. During the days of the festival, there are all sorts of events organized. All art-related and cultural events are free to attend, which makes the whole experience even more interesting.

Last, but not least, there is the Moesgård Viking Moot (http://www.moesgaardmuseum.dk/). This is organized in the town of Aarhus as well, each year, on the last weekend of July. This is a celebration of the Viking culture, with the re-creation of festive markets and archery events. The highlight of the event is the warrior battles, reminding all participants of the Viking heritage that the Danes proudly possess.

SHOP TILL YOU DROP

Denmark Shop - Photo Source: pixabay.com

Copenhagen is a paradise for shopping enthusiasts, with many shops offering both national and international brands. If you are passionate about antique shopping, you should definitely consider visiting Bredgade, one of the best shopping streets in all of Copenhagen. This street goes from Kastellet to Kongens Nytorv and, as you walk on the street, you will also pass by the Amalienborg Castle. If you want exclusive shops, this is the right street for you to visit. Start your shopping adventure with Danish Classics (http://www.danishclassic.dk). This is a beautiful shop, where you can find authentic Danish design, bearing the trademark signature of important names such as Arne Jacobsen, Poul Henningsen and Royal Copenhagen. Another interesting shop to visit is Klassisk (http://www.klassisk.dk), providing classic designs as well.

The second shopping street that is worth visiting in Copenhagen is Ravnsborgade, where you can find antique shops as well but the products are less extravagant and they certainly do not cost as much. If you are interested in department stores, you should check out Illum (http://www.illum.eu). This store has everything you could ever want when it comes to shopping, from haute couture clothing to elegant perfumes. There are plenty of shops that provide products belonging to authentic Scandinavian brands as well. Magasin du Nord (http://www.magasin/dk) is a department store as well, with a tradition that dates back all way to 1879. This is one of the best places to discover Scandinavian brands, plus it has a very nice wine shop that is worth checking out as well.

If clothes are your main subject of interest, you can pay a visit to Birger Christensen (http://www.birger-christensen.com). This has been a fashion house since 1869 and today it provides fashionable clothes from reputed brands, including Chanel, Hermes and Lanvin. Plus, it has its own fur label, which makes it even more interesting to check out. As for shoe shops, you can check out Kassandra (http://www.kassandra.dk). This shop has shoes belonging to premium fashion labels, such as Prada, Miu Miu or Stella McCartney. Apart from that, you will find an interesting variety of bags, belonging to reputed brands as well.

For a completely different shopping experience, you can go to the Dansk Design Center Shop (http://www.ddc.dk). This shop belongs to the organization with the same name, working to support the Danish design worldwide. Here, you can find an interesting selection of books and magazines, not to mention amazing gadgets. Speaking about unique experiences, a visit to the shop of Royal Copenhagen (http://www.royalcopenhagen.com) is definitely worth it. Here, you can find an interesting selection of porcelain and visit the museum located on the 2nd floor. Before Christmas, there is an annual exhibition, with celebrities using the products from Royal Copenhagen in order to decorate Christmas tables.

Not only Copenhagen is a paradise for shopping lovers but the rest of Denmark as well. In fact, in the past few years, Denmark has been often presented as one of the hottest design nations in the world. With a rich design history and important names such as Arne Jacobsen or Hans J. Wegner, it's no wonder that Denmark is leading the top when it comes to the design sector. Everywhere you travel in this amazing country, you can find unbelievable products and Scandinavian gifts that you can offer to your loved ones.

Aalborg is one of the best cities for shopping in Denmark, with both specialty and department stores. There are two main shopping streets in Aalborg, meaning Bispensgade and Algade. However, you will see that Aaalborg has so much more to offer. You can visit Nørregade and discover the works of the glass artist Lene Højlund or purchase lovely ceramics from Lange Kunsthåndværk (http://www.langekeramik.dk). You should also consider purchasing a bottle of traditional Aalborg Akvavit, which is snaps, together with special glasses or mead, which is a sweet honey drink. If you have a passion for the Viking culture, you can purchase Viking jewelry. This can be found at the Viking Museum (http://www.vikingdenmark.com), in Lindholm Høje.

Another amazing city for shopping enthusiasts who are visiting Denmark is Aarhus. As a matter of fact, Aarhus has been named as one of the best cities for shopping in the northern part of Europe. Here, you can visit ARoS (http://aros.dk), enjoying the wealth of design products belonging to both national and international brands. For a refreshing shopping experience, be sure to check out Kähler (http://www.kahlerdesign.com/). In this shop, you can experience authentic Nordic design at its finest. Seeing the product diversity, you will certainly not resist the temptation of purchasing just one product.

In case you are passionate about books, it is recommended that you pay a visit to Bog & Ide (http://www.bog-ide.dk). This is one bookstore with a tradition of 73 years, providing guide books, maps and the most interesting souvenirs. The bookshop is located near the Town Hall of Aarhus, so you won't have any difficulties trying to find it. On the other hand, if you want to shop till you drop, you can visit City Vest (http://www.cityvest.dk). This is one of the largest shopping centers in this part of Denmark, providing a wealth of shops and an unbelievable diverse food square.

There are many more other cities to explore for shopping Denmark. For example, Odense has plenty of shopping opportunities to offer as well. The town of Hans Christian Andersen entices potential shoppers with two pedestrian streets that have a high concentration of shops, meaning Kongensgade and Vestergade. In conclusion, shopping in Denmark can be a genuinely fun experience and one that you will never forget. Be sure to purchase traditional souvenirs for both you and your loved ones. There are plenty of souvenir shops located all over Denmark, so you can find a nice gift for everyone back home. Over the years, these gifts are going to transform into precious memories, that is guaranteed.

A PORTRAIT OF COPENHAGEN & DENMARK

Copenhagen Square - Photo Source: pixabay.com

Connie Nielsen said that, if Copenhagen would have been a person, it would have been beautiful, generous and elegant. This is quite true, as this is one of the best cities in the world to visit. It is the capital of Denmark and for all the right reasons, being a place where art, culture and elegant come together. This city is clean, friendly and the atmosphere is relaxing above all else. The Danes way of life is catching and, during your stay in Copenhagen, you cannot help but feel a lot like them.

Copenhagen is the best place to discover the authentic Nordic culture, whether that is reflected through its culture, the local food or the events that takes place on a regular basis. There is always something happening in Copenhagen, so you will certainly not get bored during your stay in the capital of Denmark. You will be able to attend music festivals, see opera performances live on the street and shop for Danish design. The food is going to impress with its simple and elegant taste, while the hospitality of the locals (I know that from my own experience) is going to make you feel right at home. Copenhagen is a stylish town and this is seen not only in the beautiful facades of the old buildings but also in the people who walk on the street.

Traveling to Denmark, you will have the opportunity to discover a country that is beautiful from so many points of view. There are urban cities to visit and discover, islands where you can go and enjoy nature and so many, many things in between. Music festivals are organized in bigger towns such as Aalborg or Aarhus, while Odense remains a point of interest, being associated with the famous Hans Christian Andersen. The fairytale country, as Denmark is often called, has many great things to offer. Active trips are possible as well, with nature being quite wild and beautiful in certain parts of Denmark.

Coming to Denmark, you will discover a country in which good food has a simple taste, in which friends maintain close relationships and in which the bicycle is an extension of one's personality. You will be amazed to discover how powerful the influence of the Viking heritage is still felt today in different parts of Denmark. In fact, this is an important part of your visit to this country. You can visit museums dedicated to the Viking culture, purchase jewelry that is made with symbols from that era and even attend medieval festivals, in which battles are re-created. Denmark will seduce you with all of its offerings and you will certainly want to go back, as soon as you can possibly can. Sitting at home, you will find yourself thinking about your amazing trip in Denmark and how you have had the opportunity to see one of the best countries in the world.

PS: PLEASE LEAVE YOUR REVIEW

If you reached this last page, probably this travel guide has given you some ideas about your stay in Denmark!

Would you be kind enough to leave a review for this book on Amazon? It will help other travelers to find their way through this beautiful city!

Many thanks and enjoy your trip!

THE END

Made in United States
Orlando, FL
08 December 2022

COPENHAGEN AND DENMARK FOR TRAVELERS. The total guide
The comprehensive traveling guide for all your traveling needs.
By THE TOTAL TRAVEL GUIDE COMPANY
The Best and Most Unique Copenhagen and Denmark Travel Guide

Copenhagen, the capital of Denmark, is a major point of attraction for tourists from all over the world. Approximately 8.7 million people come here each year, looking to discover the authentic Nordic culture and the Danish way of life. They are drawn to the beautiful, old buildings, the delicious food and the rich calendar of cultural events. Copenhagen is a city that is alive with passion, welcoming potential tourists with the slogan "Wonderful Copenhagen".

The majority of the tourists who come to Copenhagen also want to discover the other parts of Denmark. The whole country is beautiful to visit, with some of the most popular towns for visiting being Aalborg, Aarhus or Odense. Denmark is the country of fairytales, with Hans Christian Andersen making his influence felt event today.

The Denmark Islands are especially wonderful to visit, with old monuments and castles enticing the travelers and increasing their thirst for adventure. As a tourist in Denmark, you always have something new to discover, whether it is related to culture, art or tradition. The Viking culture is also a powerful symbol of Denmark, whether it is reflected through the medieval festivals or the jewelry that reminds of times long gone.

Let this book guide you to the many places that you must see in Copenhagen and Denmark to make this trip a life changing event. This book is filled with suggested places to stay, from budget to luxurious, places to visit, local cuisines to try, and places to shop. All these suggested itineraries have been experienced first-hand and are all highly recommended to tourists.

ISBN 9781091578814

9 781091 578814